The Mindfulness Journal

Peaces of My Day

By Sheri Mabry Bestor

Balancing Arts, a division of BestSource Inc.

www.balancingartsyoga.com

ISBN 978-0-615-80315-9

Balancing Arts

Table of Contents

A Note from the Author

The Mindfulness Journal

As you open this book, become aware of how the paper feels between your fingertips. Notice the weight of the book in your hands. Breathe in the scent of newness or any other smells that come to you. Become aware of any sounds you might be hearing. Perhaps voices, leaves blowing in the wind, or the hum of a computer. Look around and see if you notice something you wouldn't normally. Maybe the sun is slanting in through the windows in such a way that the dust specs dance through the light. Become aware of how your body feels. Bring your attention to your breath.

The exercise you just performed was simple and took only seconds. Yet in its simplicity, it was profound. It guided you to more fully experience the present moment.

What if you truly began to experience each moment fully; each sensation, each taste, each feeling-with your whole Self? How much more alive would you feel?

Being mindful isn't some new fad that will come and go. Studies in both holistic practices and modern medicine show the benefits of this way of being, and specialists realize its importance for not only health, but overall well being. Mindfulness can help instill a sense of calmness, decreasing emotional reactivity. It can increase memory and focus, enhance intuition, and even help your body transition to its ideal weight. It may improve relationships and make you feel gratitude more abundantly. Being aware with your body, mind and spirit in unity will help you to feel whole, and will allow you to be more in tune with the world around you.

Using this journal fosters a mindful state of being by recording the present moment instead of the past. The process integrates your mind with your body through the exercise of writing down thoughts onto a page in response to prompts. This encourages sensory awareness, builds neural pathways, and nurtures creativity.

Life can be hectic. Use this journal not as another to-do item, but as a simple way to pause and experience the moment. You'll not only be recording memories to reflect back on, you'll be learning how to experience life. Truly and simply. So that you can discover and enjoy the Peaces of Your Day.

My wish for you is a life fully lived, moment by moment.

Live Your Light.

Sheri

How to use this book:

Carry this journal with you, like you would a day planner. Take time to pause, breathe, and record your current experience. Just jot down a few words.

Soon, through the repetition of this simple exercise, in addition to mindfully experiencing the moments you are recording, you'll realize that having the book with you will remind you to be mindful throughout your day. And eventually it will become the way you experience more and more of life's moments.

Periodically, look back at the entries, enjoy the memories, and without judgment, note how your entries have been changing. You may notice that as you become more aware, you are able to accept moments for what they are, versus allowing thoughts of past or future to interfere with the truth of the moment.

Don't wait for the grand life events to take place to use this journal, but pull it out during those seemingly inconsequential times. Feel no pressure to respond in a certain way or to fill in every part. Simply be honest, and record what is true in the moment. There are 108 pages for you to record 108 moments.

Before you begin journaling, read through the "Preparing to Journal" section and "Sample Prompt Page." These are pages to refer back to at any time.

The additional blank space is for your creative expression. Use the space to sketch a drawing inspired by the moment, write a few lines of a poem, or compose a song. Perhaps pose a question to yourself, or record intuition that surface from within. Mindfulness fuels creative energy, so listen and record what awakens.

Preparing to Journal

Before you begin jotting down your experience, take a moment to come into the moment. This exercise is a wonderful way to center your Self at any time during the day.

Bring your attention to your breath. Breathe diaphragmatically. Belly expands on the inhale, falls back on the exhale. Bring your attention to your thoughts. When they wander, encourage your thoughts back to this moment. Bring your attention to your body. Scan through and notice sensations. Become aware of where you are holding stress in your body. Release tension from your eyebrows. Jaw. Neck. Shoulders. Arms. Hands. Back. Pelvis. Legs. Feet. Become aware of your surroundings by using your senses. Breathe in and out, experiencing the moment with your mind and body. Allow your awareness to be infused with curiosity, creativity and appreciation. Allow your Self to breathe gratitude. Embody peace.

Journal the experience of the moment.

Sample Prompt Page

Here are the prompts that will help bring you to a mindful place of being, and a brief explanation of what you might become aware of within the moment to record in the journal. Try to take your Self through each prompt. Don't force yourself to write down answers for each. Simply jot down what comes up.

This moment is...

Document where you are or why. Maybe what year, time and day it is.

I am...

Record how you are feeling as you open this book. What attitude are you bringing into this moment? Are your thoughts present? If not, where are they wandering to?

My sensory awareness...

Connect with the environment. Allow your senses to perceive in a non-verbal, intimate, direct way. What do you smell, taste, feel, hear, see?

My body awareness...

How are you breathing? How does your body feel? Where are you holding tension and where are you letting it go? Close your eyes and scan your body again, becoming aware of how your body feels in space and in relation to gravity.

My emotional awareness...

Notice your feelings. Where are you holding this emotion in your body? How would you describe it?

Unifying mind, body, breath, I feel...

Truthfully describe in a *few* words, maybe even one word, how your entire Self feels being in this moment.

A truth I'm learning / a question I have...

Sometimes, intuition comes to surface when you are in a peaceful state. Other times, a question comes to light. Don't force- just allow it to come to you. Then record.

In this moment, I'm grateful for...

You don't need a whole list, and it can be simple. What are you thankful for right now?

Live Your Light

Balancing Arts

Peaces of My Day

This moment is...

I am...

My sensory awareness...

My body awareness...

My emotional awareness...

Unifying mind, body, breath; I feel...

A truth I'm learning / a question I have...

In this moment, I'm grateful for...

Creative Expression

"You must live in the present, launch yourself on every wave, find your eternity in each moment."

~Henry David Thoreau

Peaces of My Day

This moment is...

I am...

My sensory awareness...

My body awareness...

My emotional awareness...

Unifying mind, body, breath; I feel...

A truth I'm learning / a question I have...

I'm grateful for...

Sheri Mabry Bestor

Creative Expression

Peaces of My Day

This moment is…

I am…

My sensory awareness…

My body awareness…

My emotional awareness…

Unifying mind, body, breath; I feel…

A truth I'm learning / a question I have…

I'm grateful for…

Sheri Mabry Bestor

Creative Expression

Peaces of My Day

This moment is...

I am...

My sensory awareness...

My body awareness...

My emotional awareness...

Unifying mind, body, breath; I feel...

A truth I'm learning / a question I have...

I'm grateful for...

Creative Expression

Peaces of My Day

This moment is...

I am...

My sensory awareness...

My body awareness...

My emotional awareness...

Unifying mind, body, breath; I feel...

A truth I'm learning / a question I have...

I'm grateful for...

Creative Expression

Peaces of My Day

This moment is…

I am…

My sensory awareness…

My body awareness…

My emotional awareness…

Unifying mind, body, breath; I feel…

A truth I'm learning / a question I have…

I'm grateful for…

Sheri Mabry Bestor

Creative Expression

Peaces of My Day

This moment is...

I am...

My sensory awareness...

My body awareness...

My emotional awareness...

Unifying mind, body, breath; I feel...

A truth I'm learning / a question I have...

I'm grateful for...

Creative Expression

"The secret of health for both mind and body is not to mourn for the past, worry about the future, or anticipate troubles, but to live in the present moment wisely and earnestly."

~Buddha

Peaces of My Day

This moment is...

I am...

My sensory awareness...

My body awareness...

My emotional awareness...

Unifying mind, body, breath; I feel...

A truth I'm learning / a question I have...

I'm grateful for...

Creative Expression

Peaces of My Day

This moment is…

I am…

My sensory awareness…

My body awareness…

My emotional awareness…

Unifying mind, body, breath; I feel…

A truth I'm learning / a question I have…

I'm grateful for…

Sheri Mabry Bestor

Creative Expression

Peaces of My Day

This moment is...

I am...

My sensory awareness...

My body awareness...

My emotional awareness...

Unifying mind, body, breath; I feel...

A truth I'm learning / a question I have...

I'm grateful for...

Creative Expression

Peaces of My Day

This moment is...

I am...

My sensory awareness...

My body awareness...

My emotional awareness...

Unifying mind, body, breath; I feel...

A truth I'm learning / a question I have...

I'm grateful for...

Creative Expression

Peaces of My Day

This moment is...

I am...

My sensory awareness...

My body awareness...

My emotional awareness...

Unifying mind, body, breath; I feel...

A truth I'm learning / a question I have...

I'm grateful for...

Sheri Mabry Bestor

Creative Expression

Peaces of My Day

This moment is...

I am...

My sensory awareness...

My body awareness...

My emotional awareness...

Unifying mind, body, breath; I feel...

A truth I'm learning / a question I have...

I'm grateful for...

Creative Expression

"Learn to be still in the midst of activity."

~Indirha Gandhi

Peaces of My Day

This moment is...

I am...

My sensory awareness...

My body awareness...

My emotional awareness...

Unifying mind, body, breath; I feel...

A truth I'm learning / a question I have...

I'm grateful for...

Creative Expression

Peaces of My Day

This moment is...

I am...

My sensory awareness...

My body awareness...

My emotional awareness...

Unifying mind, body, breath; I feel...

A truth I'm learning / a question I have...

I'm grateful for...

Creative Expression

Peaces of My Day

This moment is...

I am...

My sensory awareness...

My body awareness...

My emotional awareness...

Unifying mind, body, breath; I feel...

A truth I'm learning / a question I have...

I'm grateful for...

Creative Expression

Peaces of My Day

This moment is...

I am...

My sensory awareness...

My body awareness...

My emotional awareness...

Unifying mind, body, breath; I feel...

A truth I'm learning / a question I have...

I'm grateful for...

Creative Expression

Peaces of My Day

This moment is…

I am…

My sensory awareness…

My body awareness…

My emotional awareness…

Unifying mind, body, breath; I feel…

A truth I'm learning / a question I have…

I'm grateful for…

Sheri Mabry Bestor

Creative Expression

Peaces of My Day

This moment is...

I am...

My sensory awareness...

My body awareness...

My emotional awareness...

Unifying mind, body, breath; I feel...

A truth I'm learning / a question I have...

I'm grateful for...

Creative Expression

"If you want to conquer the anxiety of life, live in the moment, live in the breath."

~Amit Ray, *Om Chanting and Meditation*

Peaces of My Day

This moment is...

I am...

My sensory awareness...

My body awareness...

My emotional awareness...

Unifying mind, body, breath; I feel...

A truth I'm learning / a question I have...

I'm grateful for...

Sheri Mabry Bestor

Creative Expression

Peaces of My Day

This moment is...

I am...

My sensory awareness...

My body awareness...

My emotional awareness...

Unifying mind, body, breath; I feel...

A truth I'm learning / a question I have...

I'm grateful for...

Sheri Mabry Bestor

Creative Expression

Peaces of My Day

This moment is…

I am…

My sensory awareness…

My body awareness…

My emotional awareness…

Unifying mind, body, breath; I feel…

A truth I'm learning / a question I have…

I'm grateful for…

Creative Expression

Peaces of My Day

This moment is...

I am...

My sensory awareness...

My body awareness...

My emotional awareness...

Unifying mind, body, breath; I feel...

A truth I'm learning / a question I have...

I'm grateful for...

Creative Expression

Peaces of My Day

This moment is...

I am...

My sensory awareness...

My body awareness...

My emotional awareness...

Unifying mind, body, breath; I feel...

A truth I'm learning / a question I have...

I'm grateful for...

Sheri Mabry Bestor

Creative Expression

Peaces of My Day

This moment is...

I am...

My sensory awareness...

My body awareness...

My emotional awareness...

Unifying mind, body, breath; I feel...

A truth I'm learning / a question I have...

I'm grateful for...

Creative Expression

"The present moment is filled with joy and happiness. If you are attentive, you will see it. (21)"

~Thich Nhat Hanh, *Peace Is Every Step: The Path of Mindfulness in Everyday Life*

Peaces of My Day

This moment is...

I am...

My sensory awareness...

My body awareness...

My emotional awareness...

Unifying mind, body, breath; I feel...

A truth I'm learning / a question I have...

I'm grateful for...

Creative Expression

Peaces of My Day

This moment is…

I am…

My sensory awareness…

My body awareness…

My emotional awareness…

Unifying mind, body, breath; I feel…

A truth I'm learning / a question I have…

I'm grateful for…

Creative Expression

Peaces of My Day

This moment is…

I am…

My sensory awareness…

My body awareness…

My emotional awareness…

Unifying mind, body, breath; I feel…

A truth I'm learning / a question I have…

I'm grateful for…

Creative Expression

Peaces of My Day

This moment is...

I am...

My sensory awareness...

My body awareness...

My emotional awareness...

Unifying mind, body, breath; I feel...

A truth I'm learning / a question I have...

I'm grateful for...

Creative Expression

Peaces of My Day

This moment is...

I am...

My sensory awareness...

My body awareness...

My emotional awareness...

Unifying mind, body, breath; I feel...

A truth I'm learning / a question I have...

I'm grateful for...

Creative Expression

"Always hold fast to the present. Every situation, indeed every moment, is of infinite value, for it is the representative of a whole eternity."

~Johann Wolfgang von Goethe

Peaces of My Day

This moment is...

I am...

My sensory awareness...

My body awareness...

My emotional awareness...

Unifying mind, body, breath; I feel...

A truth I'm learning / a question I have...

I'm grateful for...

Creative Expression

Peaces of My Day

This moment is…

I am…

My sensory awareness…

My body awareness…

My emotional awareness…

Unifying mind, body, breath; I feel…

A truth I'm learning / a question I have…

I'm grateful for…

Sheri Mabry Bestor

Creative Expression

Peaces of My Day

This moment is…

I am…

My sensory awareness…

My body awareness…

My emotional awareness…

Unifying mind, body, breath; I feel…

A truth I'm learning / a question I have…

I'm grateful for…

Sheri Mabry Bestor

Creative Expression

Peaces of My Day

This moment is...

I am...

My sensory awareness...

My body awareness...

My emotional awareness...

Unifying mind, body, breath; I feel...

A truth I'm learning / a question I have...

I'm grateful for...

Creative Expression

Peaces of My Day

This moment is…

I am…

My sensory awareness…

My body awareness…

My emotional awareness…

Unifying mind, body, breath; I feel…

A truth I'm learning / a question I have…

I'm grateful for…

Creative Expression

"Walk as if you are kissing the Earth with your feet."

~Thich Nhat Hanh, *Peace Is Every Step:*
The Path of Mindfulness in Everyday Life

Peaces of My Day

This moment is…

I am…

My sensory awareness…

My body awareness…

My emotional awareness…

Unifying mind, body, breath; I feel…

A truth I'm learning / a question I have…

I'm grateful for…

Sheri Mabry Bestor

Creative Expression

Peaces of My Day

This moment is…

I am…

My sensory awareness…

My body awareness…

My emotional awareness…

Unifying mind, body, breath; I feel…

A truth I'm learning / a question I have…

I'm grateful for…

Sheri Mabry Bestor

Creative Expression

Peaces of My Day

This moment is...

I am...

My sensory awareness...

My body awareness...

My emotional awareness...

Unifying mind, body, breath; I feel...

A truth I'm learning / a question I have...

I'm grateful for...

Sheri Mabry Bestor

Creative Expression

Peaces of My Day

This moment is…

I am…

My sensory awareness…

My body awareness…

My emotional awareness…

Unifying mind, body, breath; I feel…

A truth I'm learning / a question I have…

I'm grateful for…

Creative Expression

Peaces of My Day

This moment is...

I am...

My sensory awareness...

My body awareness...

My emotional awareness...

Unifying mind, body, breath; I feel...

A truth I'm learning / a question I have...

I'm grateful for...

Creative Expression

Waking up this morning, I smile,

Twenty four brand new hours are before me.

I vow to live fully in each moment

and to look at all beings with eyes of compassion.

~Thich Nhat Hanh

Peaces of My Day

This moment is...

I am...

My sensory awareness...

My body awareness...

My emotional awareness...

Unifying mind, body, breath; I feel...

A truth I'm learning / a question I have...

I'm grateful for...

Sheri Mabry Bestor

Creative Expression

Peaces of My Day

This moment is...

I am...

My sensory awareness...

My body awareness...

My emotional awareness...

Unifying mind, body, breath; I feel...

A truth I'm learning / a question I have...

I'm grateful for...

Sheri Mabry Bestor

Creative Expression

Peaces of My Day

This moment is…

I am…

My sensory awareness…

My body awareness…

My emotional awareness…

Unifying mind, body, breath; I feel…

A truth I'm learning / a question I have…

I'm grateful for…

Sheri Mabry Bestor

Creative Expression

Peaces of My Day

This moment is…

I am…

My sensory awareness…

My body awareness…

My emotional awareness…

Unifying mind, body, breath; I feel…

A truth I'm learning / a question I have…

I'm grateful for…

Sheri Mabry Bestor

Creative Expression

Peaces of My Day

This moment is…

I am…

My sensory awareness…

My body awareness…

My emotional awareness…

Unifying mind, body, breath; I feel…

A truth I'm learning / a question I have…

I'm grateful for…

Creative Expression

"As you walk and eat and travel, be where you are. Otherwise you will miss most of your life."

~Buddha

Peaces of My Day

This moment is...

I am...

My sensory awareness...

My body awareness...

My emotional awareness...

Unifying mind, body, breath; I feel...

A truth I'm learning / a question I have...

I'm grateful for...

Creative Expression

Peaces of My Day

This moment is...

I am...

My sensory awareness...

My body awareness...

My emotional awareness...

Unifying mind, body, breath; I feel...

A truth I'm learning / a question I have...

I'm grateful for...

Sheri Mabry Bestor

Creative Expression

Peaces of My Day

This moment is…

I am…

My sensory awareness…

My body awareness…

My emotional awareness…

Unifying mind, body, breath; I feel…

A truth I'm learning / a question I have…

I'm grateful for…

Creative Expression

Peaces of My Day

This moment is...

I am...

My sensory awareness...

My body awareness...

My emotional awareness...

Unifying mind, body, breath; I feel...

A truth I'm learning / a question I have...

I'm grateful for...

Creative Expression

Peaces of My Day

This moment is…

I am…

My sensory awareness…

My body awareness…

My emotional awareness…

Unifying mind, body, breath; I feel…

A truth I'm learning / a question I have…

I'm grateful for…

Creative Expression

"Feelings come and go like clouds in a windy sky. Conscious breathing is my anchor."

~Thich Nhat Hanh, *Stepping into Freedom:*
Rules of Monastic Practice for Novices

Peaces of My Day

This moment is...

I am...

My sensory awareness...

My body awareness...

My emotional awareness...

Unifying mind, body, breath; I feel...

A truth I'm learning / a question I have...

I'm grateful for...

Creative Expression

Peaces of My Day

This moment is...

I am...

My sensory awareness...

My body awareness...

My emotional awareness...

Unifying mind, body, breath; I feel...

A truth I'm learning / a question I have...

I'm grateful for...

Creative Expression

Peaces of My Day

This moment is...

I am...

My sensory awareness...

My body awareness...

My emotional awareness...

Unifying mind, body, breath; I feel...

A truth I'm learning / a question I have...

I'm grateful for...

Creative Expression

Peaces of My Day

This moment is...

I am...

My sensory awareness...

My body awareness...

My emotional awareness...

Unifying mind, body, breath; I feel...

A truth I'm learning / a question I have...

I'm grateful for...

Creative Expression

Peaces of My Day

This moment is…

I am…

My sensory awareness…

My body awareness…

My emotional awareness…

Unifying mind, body, breath; I feel…

A truth I'm learning / a question I have…

I'm grateful for…

Creative Expression

"The way to live in the present is to remember that "This too shall pass." When you experience joy, remembering that "This too shall pass" helps you savor the here and now. When you experience pain and sorrow, remembering that "This too shall pass" reminds you that grief, like joy, is only temporary."

~Joey Green

Peaces of My Day

This moment is...

I am...

My sensory awareness...

My body awareness...

My emotional awareness...

Unifying mind, body, breath; I feel...

A truth I'm learning / a question I have...

I'm grateful for...

Creative Expression

Peaces of My Day

This moment is…

I am…

My sensory awareness…

My body awareness…

My emotional awareness…

Unifying mind, body, breath; I feel…

A truth I'm learning / a question I have…

I'm grateful for…

Sheri Mabry Bestor

Creative Expression

Peaces of My Day

This moment is...

I am...

My sensory awareness...

My body awareness...

My emotional awareness...

Unifying mind, body, breath; I feel...

A truth I'm learning / a question I have...

I'm grateful for...

Sheri Mabry Bestor

Creative Expression

Peaces of My Day

This moment is...

I am...

My sensory awareness...

My body awareness...

My emotional awareness...

Unifying mind, body, breath; I feel...

A truth I'm learning / a question I have...

I'm grateful for...

Creative Expression

Peaces of My Day

This moment is...

I am...

My sensory awareness...

My body awareness...

My emotional awareness...

Unifying mind, body, breath; I feel...

A truth I'm learning / a question I have...

I'm grateful for...

Creative Expression

"Gratitude unlocks the fullness of life."

~Melody Beattie

Peaces of My Day

This moment is...

I am...

My sensory awareness...

My body awareness...

My emotional awareness...

Unifying mind, body, breath; I feel...

A truth I'm learning / a question I have...

I'm grateful for...

Creative Expression

Peaces of My Day

This moment is…

I am…

My sensory awareness…

My body awareness…

My emotional awareness…

Unifying mind, body, breath; I feel…

A truth I'm learning / a question I have…

I'm grateful for…

Creative Expression

Peaces of My Day

This moment is...

I am...

My sensory awareness...

My body awareness...

My emotional awareness...

Unifying mind, body, breath; I feel...

A truth I'm learning / a question I have...

I'm grateful for...

Sheri Mabry Bestor

Creative Expression

Peaces of My Day

This moment is...

I am...

My sensory awareness...

My body awareness...

My emotional awareness...

Unifying mind, body, breath; I feel...

A truth I'm learning / a question I have...

I'm grateful for...

Creative Expression

Peaces of My Day

This moment is…

I am…

My sensory awareness…

My body awareness…

My emotional awareness…

Unifying mind, body, breath; I feel…

A truth I'm learning / a question I have…

I'm grateful for…

Sheri Mabry Bestor

Creative Expression

Peaces of My Day

This moment is…

I am…

My sensory awareness…

My body awareness…

My emotional awareness…

Unifying mind, body, breath; I feel…

A truth I'm learning / a question I have…

I'm grateful for…

Creative Expression

"If you concentrate on finding whatever is good in every situation, you will discover that your life will suddenly be filled with gratitude, a feeling that nurtures the soul."

~Rabbi Harold Kushner

Peaces of My Day

This moment is...

I am...

My sensory awareness...

My body awareness...

My emotional awareness...

Unifying mind, body, breath; I feel...

A truth I'm learning / a question I have...

I'm grateful for...

Creative Expression

Peaces of My Day

This moment is...

I am...

My sensory awareness...

My body awareness...

My emotional awareness...

Unifying mind, body, breath; I feel...

A truth I'm learning / a question I have...

I'm grateful for...

Creative Expression

Peaces of My Day

This moment is...

I am...

My sensory awareness...

My body awareness...

My emotional awareness...

Unifying mind, body, breath; I feel...

A truth I'm learning / a question I have...

I'm grateful for...

Creative Expression

Peaces of My Day

This moment is...

I am...

My sensory awareness...

My body awareness...

My emotional awareness...

Unifying mind, body, breath; I feel...

A truth I'm learning / a question I have...

I'm grateful for...

Sheri Mabry Bestor

Creative Expression

Peaces of My Day

This moment is...

I am...

My sensory awareness...

My body awareness...

My emotional awareness...

Unifying mind, body, breath; I feel...

A truth I'm learning / a question I have...

I'm grateful for...

Creative Expression

"Be content with what you have;

Rejoice in the way things are.

When you realize there is nothing lacking,

The whole world belongs to you."

~Lao Tzu

Peaces of My Day

This moment is…

I am…

My sensory awareness…

My body awareness…

My emotional awareness…

Unifying mind, body, breath; I feel…

A truth I'm learning / a question I have…

I'm grateful for…

Sheri Mabry Bestor

Creative Expression

Peaces of My Day

This moment is...

I am...

My sensory awareness...

My body awareness...

My emotional awareness...

Unifying mind, body, breath; I feel...

A truth I'm learning / a question I have...

I'm grateful for...

Creative Expression

Peaces of My Day

This moment is...

I am...

My sensory awareness...

My body awareness...

My emotional awareness...

Unifying mind, body, breath; I feel...

A truth I'm learning / a question I have...

I'm grateful for...

Creative Expression

Peaces of My Day

This moment is...

I am...

My sensory awareness...

My body awareness...

My emotional awareness...

Unifying mind, body, breath; I feel...

A truth I'm learning / a question I have...

I'm grateful for...

Sheri Mabry Bestor

Creative Expression

Peaces of My Day

This moment is...

I am...

My sensory awareness...

My body awareness...

My emotional awareness...

Unifying mind, body, breath; I feel...

A truth I'm learning / a question I have...

I'm grateful for...

Sheri Mabry Bestor

Creative Expression

Peaces of My Day

This moment is…

I am…

My sensory awareness…

My body awareness…

My emotional awareness…

Unifying mind, body, breath; I feel…

A truth I'm learning / a question I have…

I'm grateful for…

Creative Expression

"There's only one reason why you're not experiencing bliss at this present moment, and it's because you're thinking or focusing on what you don't have…But, right now you have everything you need to be in bliss."

~Anthony de Mello

Peaces of My Day

This moment is...

I am...

My sensory awareness...

My body awareness...

My emotional awareness...

Unifying mind, body, breath; I feel...

A truth I'm learning / a question I have...

I'm grateful for...

Sheri Mabry Bestor

Creative Expression

Peaces of My Day

This moment is...

I am...

My sensory awareness...

My body awareness...

My emotional awareness...

Unifying mind, body, breath; I feel...

A truth I'm learning / a question I have...

I'm grateful for...

Sheri Mabry Bestor

Creative Expression

Peaces of My Day

This moment is…

I am…

My sensory awareness…

My body awareness…

My emotional awareness…

Unifying mind, body, breath; I feel…

A truth I'm learning / a question I have…

I'm grateful for…

Creative Expression

Peaces of My Day

This moment is...

I am...

My sensory awareness...

My body awareness...

My emotional awareness...

Unifying mind, body, breath; I feel...

A truth I'm learning / a question I have...

I'm grateful for...

Sheri Mabry Bestor

Creative Expression

Peaces of My Day

This moment is…

I am…

My sensory awareness…

My body awareness…

My emotional awareness…

Unifying mind, body, breath; I feel…

A truth I'm learning / a question I have…

I'm grateful for…

Creative Expression

"Be happy for this moment. This moment is your life"

~Omar Kayyám

Peaces of My Day

This moment is...

I am...

My sensory awareness...

My body awareness...

My emotional awareness...

Unifying mind, body, breath; I feel...

A truth I'm learning / a question I have...

I'm grateful for...

Sheri Mabry Bestor

Creative Expression

Peaces of My Day

This moment is...

I am...

My sensory awareness...

My body awareness...

My emotional awareness...

Unifying mind, body, breath; I feel...

A truth I'm learning / a question I have...

I'm grateful for...

Sheri Mabry Bestor

Creative Expression

Peaces of My Day

This moment is...

I am...

My sensory awareness...

My body awareness...

My emotional awareness...

Unifying mind, body, breath; I feel...

A truth I'm learning / a question I have...

I'm grateful for...

Creative Expression

Peaces of My Day

This moment is...

I am...

My sensory awareness...

My body awareness...

My emotional awareness...

Unifying mind, body, breath; I feel...

A truth I'm learning / a question I have...

I'm grateful for...

Creative Expression

Peaces of My Day

This moment is…

I am…

My sensory awareness…

My body awareness…

My emotional awareness…

Unifying mind, body, breath; I feel…

A truth I'm learning / a question I have…

I'm grateful for…

Sheri Mabry Bestor

Creative Expression

Peaces of My Day

This moment is...

I am...

My sensory awareness...

My body awareness...

My emotional awareness...

Unifying mind, body, breath; I feel...

A truth I'm learning / a question I have...

I'm grateful for...

Creative Expression

"I said to my soul, be still, and wait...So the darkness shall be the light, and the stillness the dancing."

~T.S. Eliot

Peaces of My Day

This moment is...

I am...

My sensory awareness...

My body awareness...

My emotional awareness...

Unifying mind, body, breath; I feel...

A truth I'm learning / a question I have...

I'm grateful for...

Creative Expression

Peaces of My Day

This moment is…

I am…

My sensory awareness…

My body awareness…

My emotional awareness…

Unifying mind, body, breath; I feel…

A truth I'm learning / a question I have…

I'm grateful for…

Creative Expression

Peaces of My Day

This moment is...

I am...

My sensory awareness...

My body awareness...

My emotional awareness...

Unifying mind, body, breath; I feel...

A truth I'm learning / a question I have...

I'm grateful for...

Creative Expression

Peaces of My Day

This moment is...

I am...

My sensory awareness...

My body awareness...

My emotional awareness...

Unifying mind, body, breath; I feel...

A truth I'm learning / a question I have...

I'm grateful for...

Creative Expression

Peaces of My Day

This moment is...

I am...

My sensory awareness...

My body awareness...

My emotional awareness...

Unifying mind, body, breath; I feel...

A truth I'm learning / a question I have...

I'm grateful for...

Creative Expression

"Once you stop clinging and let things be, you'll be free, even of birth and death. You'll transform everything…And you'll be at peace wherever you are."

~Bodhidharma

Peaces of My Day

This moment is...

I am...

My sensory awareness...

My body awareness...

My emotional awareness...

Unifying mind, body, breath; I feel...

A truth I'm learning / a question I have...

I'm grateful for...

Sheri Mabry Bestor

Creative Expression

Peaces of My Day

This moment is…

I am…

My sensory awareness…

My body awareness…

My emotional awareness…

Unifying mind, body, breath; I feel…

A truth I'm learning / a question I have…

I'm grateful for…

Creative Expression

Peaces of My Day

This moment is…

I am…

My sensory awareness…

My body awareness…

My emotional awareness…

Unifying mind, body, breath; I feel…

A truth I'm learning / a question I have…

I'm grateful for…

Sheri Mabry Bestor

Creative Expression

Peaces of My Day

This moment is...

I am...

My sensory awareness...

My body awareness...

My emotional awareness...

Unifying mind, body, breath; I feel...

A truth I'm learning / a question I have...

I'm grateful for...

Creative Expression

Peaces of My Day

This moment is...

I am...

My sensory awareness...

My body awareness...

My emotional awareness...

Unifying mind, body, breath; I feel...

A truth I'm learning / a question I have...

I'm grateful for...

Creative Expression

"Let the beauty we love be what we do; there are hundreds of ways to kneel and kiss the ground."

~Rumi

Peaces of My Day

This moment is...

I am...

My sensory awareness...

My body awareness...

My emotional awareness...

Unifying mind, body, breath; I feel...

A truth I'm learning / a question I have...

I'm grateful for...

Creative Expression

Peaces of My Day

This moment is...

I am...

My sensory awareness...

My body awareness...

My emotional awareness...

Unifying mind, body, breath; I feel...

A truth I'm learning / a question I have...

I'm grateful for...

Creative Expression

Peaces of My Day

This moment is...

I am...

My sensory awareness...

My body awareness...

My emotional awareness...

Unifying mind, body, breath; I feel...

A truth I'm learning / a question I have...

I'm grateful for...

Creative Expression

Peaces of My Day

This moment is…

I am…

My sensory awareness…

My body awareness…

My emotional awareness…

Unifying mind, body, breath; I feel…

A truth I'm learning / a question I have…

I'm grateful for…

Creative Expression

Peaces of My Day

This moment is...

I am...

My sensory awareness...

My body awareness...

My emotional awareness...

Unifying mind, body, breath; I feel...

A truth I'm learning / a question I have...

I'm grateful for...

Creative Expression

"Breathing in, I calm body and mind. Breathing out, I smile. Dwelling in the present moment I know this is the only moment."

~Thich Nhat Hanh, *Being Peace*

Peaces of My Day

This moment is...

I am...

My sensory awareness...

My body awareness...

My emotional awareness...

Unifying mind, body, breath; I feel...

A truth I'm learning / a question I have...

I'm grateful for...

Sheri Mabry Bestor

Creative Expression

Peaces of My Day

This moment is...

I am...

My sensory awareness...

My body awareness...

My emotional awareness...

Unifying mind, body, breath; I feel...

A truth I'm learning / a question I have...

I'm grateful for...

Sheri Mabry Bestor

Creative Expression

Peaces of My Day

This moment is...

I am...

My sensory awareness...

My body awareness...

My emotional awareness...

Unifying mind, body, breath; I feel...

A truth I'm learning / a question I have...

I'm grateful for...

Creative Expression

Peaces of My Day

This moment is...

I am...

My sensory awareness...

My body awareness...

My emotional awareness...

Unifying mind, body, breath; I feel...

A truth I'm learning / a question I have...

I'm grateful for...

Sheri Mabry Bestor

Creative Expression

Peaces of My Day

This moment is…

I am…

My sensory awareness…

My body awareness…

My emotional awareness…

Unifying mind, body, breath; I feel…

A truth I'm learning / a question I have…

I'm grateful for…

Sheri Mabry Bestor

Creative Expression

Peaces of My Day

This moment is...

I am...

My sensory awareness...

My body awareness...

My emotional awareness...

Unifying mind, body, breath; I feel...

A truth I'm learning / a question I have...

I'm grateful for...

Creative Expression

"Live your light."

~Sheri M. Bestor

Sheri Mabry Bestor is a member of Society of Children's Books Writers and Illustrators and a published book author. She has worked as a freelance writer for local newspapers and magazines and has sold work locally and nationally to magazines.

Sheri earned her BS in elementary education from the University of Wisconsin, Madison, and her MA in curriculum and instruction. She is an experienced elementary teacher, tennis instructor, drama instructor, and theater director. She is a yoga instructor certified by the Himalayan Teachers Association and a registered yoga instructor through Yoga Alliance. She is a guide for yoga and somatic movement methods, as well as a Reiki master.

Sheri is the founder and president of North Shore Academy of the Arts, Inc., a not-for-profit organization offering quality opportunities in the visual, performing, and literary arts. She is the owner of Balancing Arts, a yoga and well-being studio.

Sheri lives with her family in a small town in the Midwest.

www.sheribestor.com